This Ridiculous Life

Becky Mayhew

First published in England in 2014 by

Becky Mayhew

www.beckysaysthings.com

beckysaysthings@gmail.com

First edition: December 2014

A catalogue record of this book is available from the British Library.

ISBN: 978-0-9931425-0-5

Front cover design: Becky Mayhew and Dan Frau
Design editors: Becky Mayhew and Dan Frau

Printed by the lovely people at imprintdigital.com

For Mum and Dad.

Thank you.

Oh, GOSH.

Dear Reader, I am SO excited about welcoming you to my little book, that I fear my sentiments shall become jumbled; so, I shall structure my thoughts into a list, because I *love* a list.

1) Good day to you, my Reader. My friend. My name is Becky. Hello.

2) Thank you from the bottom of my heart for purchasing my little book. If you have not purchased my little book, then you are either a very lucky Reader for being given it by a friend, or you are a thief.

3) I write a blog called beckysaysthings.com. On this blog I say things about the peculiar and often ridiculous concept of Life. And what a ridiculous Life, Reader! It is fraught with peril, embarrassment, confusion, and the occasional walk into a lamppost.

4) This little book is an edited, spruced up and very pretty collection of some of the things I've said on my blog, as well as some *new* things that I wanted to say especially for this tome.

5) It is a journey through the oddities of Life; and, as my new pal, I would like to take you with me. Come, and experience the joy, pain, and general discomfort of human existence. Will you come? Yes? Hurrah!

6) I think we're going to get on **famously**, you and I. Perhaps at the end of our journey we could grab a drink, go to a petting zoo, play some hoopla... No? Too soon? Yeah, you're right, maybe we should just see how it goes, start off with pizza and an owl sanctuary...

AHEM RIGHT LET'S JUST GET ON WITH IT, SHALL WE?

The world of work

Becky says things about ...

... commuting

To commence, a fun multiple choice for you, my lovely new friend. Would you rather:

a) Peel off your cheek, rub salt into the bloody gaping wound, then staple the skin back onto your now irreversibly deformed face;

b) Crawl inside the anus of an elephant who is suffering from what his keeper calls 'a wobbly tummy'; or

c) Stand in a confined space with your face inside the armpit of a stranger, and breathe in the gasses and vapours of a hundred other people in the same confined space for an indeterminate amount of time, twice a day?

If you have opted for a) or b), you are most likely a commuter.

Commuting is God's way of telling you to work from home. It is the Olympics of human resilience.

If, like me, you are not blessed with height, you spend much of your commuting time standing below the heavily breathing noses of people taller than you, which can have dire effects on one's hairstyle.

You may try to read a book. However, due to the offensive proximity of 2,503,967 other people, this doesn't always work out.

Example of failed reading attempt #1

Example of failed reading attempt #2

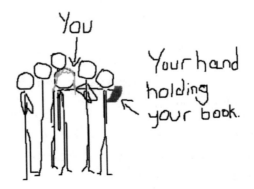

You

Your hand holding your book.

It is a territorial nightmare. You turn your head to the right and your eyeball brushes against the eyeball of a hedge fund manager from Guildford. You turn your head to the left, and the consultant dermatologist chewing gum over your shoulder accidentally bites off your nose. You learn to execute everyday actions within a minute fraction of their normal requirements: for example, sliding an object out of your bag with a movement invisible to the naked eye; holding your phone against your retina in order to text. These critical restrictions on space carry potential dangers, like the time my headphone wire got caught in the spokes of my umbrella as I was trying to fold it away, and my head ended up being sucked into my handbag.

Oh dear God.

And what if a song that you don't like comes on your iPod? Or if the volume is UNBELIEVABLY LOUD AND IS LITERALLY RIPPING YOUR EARDRUMS TO SHREDS AND WILL CAUSE YOU UNTOLD AURAL DAMAGE FOR THE REST OF YOUR LIFE? You are powerless. One of your hands is wedged against the testicles of an overweight middle manager, and the other is pinned to your side by an editorial assistant carrying a suitcase full of back issues of *Horse and Hound* magazine.

I once entered a train carriage to be faced with a man's backpack. It was preventing me from getting my whole body into the train, which is often necessary for a safe journey. I politely asked the man to take off his backpack. The man gave me a cold, hard stare, the key message of which was 'I'll wear my backpack wherever the fuck I like,' but there were palpable undertones of 'When you die, I will not only give an incorrect church address to your mourners, but I will visit your grave and write disparaging things about you on your headstone.'

I was thus forced to hope that my body was mostly inside the carriage, and as the doors closed I was relieved to discover that I had not lost a crucial appendage – and less relieved to discover that my hair had become trapped in the door. This unfortunate incident forced my head to lift towards the ceiling as the shutting doors pulled at my ponytail, and I had to spend the entire journey gazing quizzically aloft and pretending I was thinking very deeply about something and not follically shackled to a train door with some tosser's backpack wedged against my face.

Unbelievable.

Commuting is like being thrown into a room with all the ghastly things about human beings that you already hate. Incessant clearing of throats. Heavy breathing. Sniffing. Squelchy chewing. Random and inexplicable grunting. Loud domestic chats about Sebastian's unreliable cornet tutor or Roger's worsening sciatica, or loud business conversations filled with buzzwords and acronyms that make you want to vomit into your sleeve.

And our reward for a morning of psychological and physical abuse?

Work.

Brilliant.

Becky says things about ...
... the first day of a new job

Let me tell you a story, my precious. A story of fear.

I walk into a coffee shop. There is a young girl behind the counter. We look at each other. The girl has **TRAINEE BARISTA** emblazoned on her shirt. I realise I am looking into the face of terror.

It almost feels cruel ordering coffee from her.

She handles the equipment as though it is made from the finest crystal; pours the milk into the jug like it is the puréed remains of Christ himself, and when she spills the tiniest globule onto the counter, she looks at me as though I am going to club her to death with an almond croissant. When she whispers 'I'm so sorry – it's my first day,' I want to hug her.

Because, dear Reader, is there any fear like the first day of a new job?

My first ever day of work at the age of 15 was at a backstreet telesales company that sold double glazing. I was presented with a sticky phone, a soiled phonebook, a chewed pencil, a dubiously stained script, and a deep sense of everything in the world being black and wretched.

I was told to call members of the public and sell them double glazing. I stared at my besmirched equipment and suddenly realised that I had an insurmountable phobia of phones, the public, and talking. Given the choice of phoning a stranger and trying to sell them substandard double glazing, or sandpapering my own corneas, my decision would have been swift.

After 20 minutes of trying to devise a cunning and elaborate escape, I pulled myself together, dialled the first number, and had a conversation with a member of the English public that went thus:

'Hi, my name's Becky – I'm not trying to sell you anything, but – '

'If you call me again I will hunt you down and I will kill you.'

On my first day of working in a gift shop when I was 16, I realised I had a terrible fear of greetings cards. Oh, Readerbobs, they all look harmless when they're neatly stacked in their displays, but when you're the poor chump who has to get them out of their box, find their slots, price them, and stock-check them against a mystifying coding system that was devised by an alcoholic Mathematician in a subterranean lair, it is distressing.

'Happy Birthday' — E22.
'Get Well Soon' — 71Y.
'Congratulations' — 4D-G.

I want my mum.

After emerging from the emotional persecution of greetings cards, I was handed a duster and told to dust the shelves. As a result, I discovered a snippet of wisdom that is invaluable for your first day in a new job: find a task that you can do and do it **very slowly** and **very thoroughly**, thereby keeping well out of the deep water of responsibility and remaining safely in your comfort zone.

I dusted well. I dusted with gusto. I dusted for three hours, cowering every time a customer came near me – until the worst fear of anyone on their first day in retail was realised: **SOMEONE ASKED ME A QUESTION.**

I thus learnt my second piece of wisdom: people are generally stupid.

What about your first day in an office, Becky? I hear you ask. Patience, my love. I will tell.

If you are unfortunate enough to be taking over somebody else's job, starting work in an office is like bursting in on a recently-bereaved family, grabbing the urn off the mantelpiece, and shitting in it.

Your desk is not your own. It is the desk of Val, the adored colleague who sat there before you. On that first day, and for a fair time thereafter, you are The Person Who Took Val's Job. You are writing with Val's pencil. You are stapling with Val's stapler. You open Val's desk drawer to find an old coffee mug filled with some form of decomposing matter, and you innocently hold it up and say 'Is this anyone's?', and the office sinks into a stony, grieving silence, and you know that you are not welcome in their village.

But there is no fear comparable to your first day as a bartender.

I was 20. I walked behind the bar on my first shift to be confronted with the faces of six men behind a gauze of smoke. I couldn't have felt more exposed if I had pulled down my knickers and straddled the beer pumps.

The landlord placed me two feet away from the group of men, wrapped his arms around me, put his hand over mine on the beer pump, and pulled it down, all the while murmuring '*Theeeeeere* we go, pull it *hhaaaaarrrd*, don't be afraid of it, give it a good *tug*, now,' while the men viewed me in solemnly judging silence. Uncomfortable? Yes, darling. Exorbitantly.

I spent my first shift staring numbly at the ludicrous number of bottles, the baffling mass of glasses, and wondering if I could make it through my entire barmaiding career without ever having to serve anyone a drink.

The *exposure*, Reader. Oh, certainly, in *Space* no one can hear you scream, but behind a bar *everyone* can hear you scream, and *everyone* can hear when you drop a glass and *everyone* can see when your skirt's tucked into your knickers and *everyone* can see when you're staring at the shelves trying *desperately* to see the brandy and pretending *desperately* that you're *not* desperately trying to see the brandy, and there is **no escape.** Space is a walk in the park.

Fortunately for the girl in the coffee shop, it would have got easier. She would have become more confident and more assured, until she wondered what she was ever worried about. She would also have developed a comforting abhorrence of humanity and everything it stands for, and that's just the beauty of life.

Becky says things about ...
... monstrous things about working in an office

Do you work in an office, my little dumpling? Yes? No? Not sure? (If you're not sure, I suggest you rethink your suitability to the workplace in general.) If you work in an office, as I have done for several years, then you will understand that it holds many joys. To name but a few:

- Office banter (I once mused out loud 'What's my email password?' and my boss replied "I'm a fuckwit'?')
- Office pranks (who *doesn't* enjoy covering their colleague's desk with pictures of Alan Titchmarsh?)
- Office cakes (raspberry lamington from Jean in Finance, anyone?)
- Unbridled access to lots and lots of stationery

Yep, working in an office can be an absolute treat.

HOWEVER.

There are some truly monstrous things about working in an office. Things that make you want to lock yourself in the stationery cupboard with a copy of *Mein Kampf* and some ketamine.

The Toilets

Now, I cannot speak for you gents. I do not frequent the men's toilets and thus can't make scathing remarks about your sanitation habits. However, I am extremely qualified to be scathing about the ladies' toilets.

Picture this: you have been on the phone for an hour and your bladder is perilously close to bursting. You finally get off the phone, sprint to the toilets, and are faced with this:

That's right. The woman who used this toilet before you deemed it appropriate – necessary, even – to defy social convention and wee *on* the toilet instead of *in* the toilet. Yes, menfolk, it's not just you who suffer the odd wayward wee. The sight you see above happens ALL. THE. TIME.

But understand this: **I know who the culprits are.** They are The Crouchers. The women who cannot bear to have their delicate behinds touch the odious filth of the toilet seat.

I have three things to say to The Crouchers:

1) The toilet seat was not odiously filthy before you crouched over it to avoid touching its odious filthiness. It became odiously filthy after you crouched over it to avoid its odious filthiness. Do not crouch. Your wee will go wayward. You are odiously filthy.

2) Unless you are an odiously filthy fiend from the netherworlds, you would never, ever be okay with leaving your own toilet in your own house in that odious state. That is how people die. Clean it the hell up.

3) Your wee is always, without fail, this colour:

You are not drinking enough water. Drink some water.

Non-Responders

You send an email to someone who will supposedly be able to help with your query, or give you the endorsement or authorisation that you require in order to fulfil your next task. You are peeved at a non-response within 24 hours. At 48 hours you are wishing a pestilence on their family. At 179 hours, you send them this email:

Dear Spawn of the Antichrist

Please highlight the reason as to why you are not responding to my email.

1 – You are a lazy incompetent oik who is just hanging on for the pension and a bungalow in Scarborough, and thus don't give a pig's widdle about your job or your colleagues associated therein.

2 – You're terrified of taking responsibility for anything, and have deemed it safer to pretend you did not receive my email, and that I was never born.

3 – You are far too important to respond directly to lowly administrators, and will instead treat my obnoxious missive with the silence it deserves.

4 – You are dead.

If the reason is 4, good. The world is a better place without your loathsome insolence. If the answer is 1, 2 or 3, answer my fucking email you miserably inept little worm.

Kind regards

Becky

They still won't respond.

Running Commentaries on Daily Activities

Every office has a colleague who lacks an interior monologue. They tell you everything: how many emails they have in their inbox, how they have responded to said emails, which documents they have just printed, their intention to retrieve said documents from the printer, and how they are waiting for someone to respond to an email.

SHUT UP OR I WILL
HOLE PUNCH YOUR EYELIDS.

You are not at Speaker's Corner. Learn to think in your own horrid head.

Elitist Managers

There are people in this world who are so *unfathomably important,* so *incredibly high up in the hierarchy of crucial human beings,* without whom the economy would *literally implode.* Those elusive, faceless names that float over your organisation like myths. If anyone claims to have actually *met* this phantom, the rest of your office goes 'What? She *exists*? I thought she was made-up, like Aslan.'

And if you are fortunate enough to get your grubby mitts on a direct number to this ivory tower, they will speak to you like this:

'Excuse me, who *are* you? How did you get my number? Have you gone through my PA, Linda? How dare you call me directly! You need to go through Linda, my PA. That's my PA, Linda. And even then, because I'm so inconceivably important, I will grant you only a 90-second audience in three and a half years' time, and that will be over Skype from my chalet in Switzerland. But my PA, Linda, will organise it.'

There is no justification for such arrogance. Just imagine how these people speak to their partners?

What do you
think you're
doing? Have
you gone
through Linda?

Get real, you pompous swine. You go home and cry into a packet of foie gras, I go home and smile into a Fisherman's Pie. Power to the people!

Long Voicemails

You come in on a Monday morning and pick up this voicemail:

'Hi, it's Barry. I'm just after a quick catch-up on the mousemat situation...'

THREE HOURS OF VOICEMAIL FROM BARRY

'...anyway, give me a buzz when you get this and we'll chat about it.'

Please, Barry.

'Hi, it's Barry. Give me a call back when you can,' will suffice. Listen to me, Barry. Life's too short.

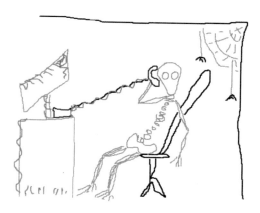

Technology

Our world is very high-tech. Isn't it great? We don't need to use pens anymore, we can send messages across the world at the click of a button, we can print documents using our phones, we can do anything. Anything! Except that we can't.

Namely, by the fridge or in the toilets. How many times have you been frightened to retrieve your salad from the kitchen because these people are standing right in front of the fridge?

And why do people choose to reveal their deepest secrets in the toilets? The office is no place for lavatorial revelations. I appreciate that you may be concerned about your son's marijuana habit – although you should be grateful it's not heroin or caviar (expensive) – but when I go to the toilet at work I do not want to hear your in-depth conversation, just like you do not want to hear me tinkle. I'd like to tinkle in private, thank you very much. Hearing about your son's marijuana addiction a foot away from me as I sit on the toilet gives me stage fright, and I will just have to sit there not tinkling until you leave.

I wouldn't mind, but
he just sits in his
room eating.

My angel, it's been a painful journey of monstrous situations, many of which you may have experienced only today. And you will experience them again tomorrow. And the next day. And the next and the next, until you retire, when you shall yearn every day for a monstrous office situation to enliven the eternal barren monotony of your twilight years.

Becky says things about ...
... meetings

Oh, Readerpops.

Meetings.

They are an integral part of adult life, like love, binge-eating Doritos, and buying the wrong bin bags. Whatever your vocation in this bewildering grown-up world, you will, most likely, have sat through a meeting.

That meeting might have been so phenomenal that you emerged from it on a PowerPoint-induced high and were forced to expend the adrenaline by going to an all-you-can-eat Chinese buffet or doing a bungee-jump.

Sorry guys, but I've just been to a residents' meeting and I am pumped.

On the other hand, that meeting may have caused you to question the very meaning of humanity, wish a serious 'accident' upon everyone in the room, and wonder whether the fall from the window would kill you.

Bollocks

The question 'Why are meetings evil?' is one of the most pressing and profound in the modern world, and I have attempted to answer it with a comprehensive list of reasons; and, for the good of mankind, have also suggested the best remedies with which to combat these ghastly situations.

Content

Content is the foundation behind the evilness of any meeting. I bet you ten English pounds that you have never sat down at a large cluster of tables with a plastic cup of cold coffee and been told 'The purpose of today's meeting is to design a Julie Andrews-themed amusement park, and to come up with names for rides, like 'Supercalifragilisticgoodnessmethisisfast'. We will also be drawing a lot of pictures of roller coasters.'

That literally never happens.

Instead, someone says 'BLAAAAAAAAA QUALITY DATA BLAAAAAAA PERFORMANCE INDICATORS BLAAAAAAA SPREADSHEETS BLAAAAAAAA EFFICIENCY MANAGEMENT BLAAAAAAAA THINK OUTSIDE THE BOX BLAAAAAAAABUMBUMBOODLEBOODLEBUM MOVING FORWARD.'

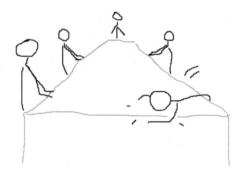

Due to the fact that the topic under discussion is invariably as enchanting as a hernia, the very act of staying alive can become a strain. You begin to wish your skin would melt off just so you could leave the room to go to the First Aid Box. The speaker's words become simply noises, like a walrus humming. You worry that your brain is dissolving and will soon dribble out of your ears like a torrent of porridge. The clock says that you have two more hours to endure, and you panic.

Remedy

If there is a view from the window, estimate how long it would take you to travel from one end of the view to the other using various styles of movement e.g. crawling, galloping, ambling as though filled with hubris. If there is no view from the window, imagine one bursting with sunshine, meadows, and those cartoon cupids from *Fantasia*. If there is no window, leave immediately. You are being held against your will and they are going to torture you, remove your limbs, and laugh at your helpless torso.

Room Temperature

In an age where we can hold the world in our hands, explore distant galaxies, and make washing machines that are also tumble dryers, *no one* has invented a meeting room with a stable climate. In these chambers of atmospheric whimsy you will either be boiled to death in temperatures that would make cacti ask for a glass of water, or you will contract hypothermia in a polar vortex about which you can do absolutely NOTHING. Why?

Because the air-conditioning is controlled from an office in Bishops Stortford, and by the time you have logged a call, requested that the air-conditioning be turned off, received an acknowledgement of your request and a promise to respond within 24 hours, you will already be dead.

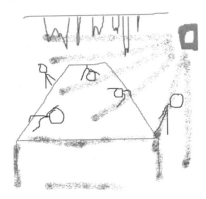

Remedy

If it is too hot, strip to your underwear, lie on the table and ask the speaker for a Lemon Fanta and a massage. If it is too cold, your most judicious option is to make a hefty coat from the skins of your colleagues.

Human Noises

Without doubt the most evil element of any meeting. In that inescapable tomb of misery, you are subjected to the bodily clanks and clunks of people up with whom you have not chosen to be locked (yes, that *is* the correct grammar, thank you, you sceptical little sausage) – because why would you *choose* to be locked up with someone who clears their throat every six and a half seconds? They don't cough, sweetness – there is apparently an insufficient build-up of phlegm to warrant an actual *cough* – they just clear their throat. A little 'hahhugm'. Every six and a half seconds. After two hours, each 'hahhugm' is like a dagger in your heart.

And then you must contend with the sniffers, sneezers, sighers and – the Godfather of all evil meeting elements – the speaker's mouth noises.

His loud swallows, like a bag of slimy marbles dropped through a gutter. The sucking of his tongue on his teeth every time he draws breath; the occasional slurp or snort; the accumulation of such a quantity of saliva in his mouth that it sounds like he's talking through a gobfull of cotton wool, and this only serves to intensify your growing panic as you begin to rock back and forth, a tear forms in your eye, and you silently offer up your own grandmother in exchange for just ONE SWALLOW.

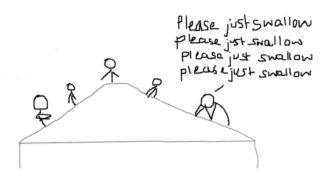

Remedy

The only way to deal with this evil meeting element is to make barbaric use of staple guns and shredding machines.

Epic Fatigue

It is well-known that meeting rooms are fitted with devices that spray invisible yet potent soporific gasses into the atmosphere to induce coma-level drowsiness. You might think you're a virile, bounding sort of chap – you eat a lot of pulses and lean protein, you fit in a couple of 5K runs a week, and people say things like 'I wish I had your energy' – but you are no match for the narcotic vapour contained inside a meeting room.

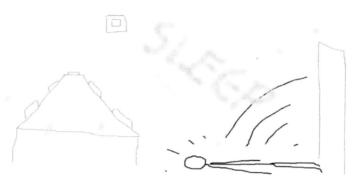

Remedy

There are two effective methods to combat epic fatigue: the first is to make a cocktail of espresso, high-energy drink, chocolate and cocaine, and 15 minutes before the meeting inject it into your eyeballs. There are possible extraordinary side-effects of this method, including re-enacting all the battle scenes from *Gladiator*, trying to walk on the ceiling, and death.

The second, less disruptive method is to simply give in to the epic fatigue and get an hour's kip. (NB: This carries a marginal risk of shouting out potentially compromising dream words.)

I hope you now feel equipped, dearest Readerpie, to deal with any future meetings that you will inevitably have to attend if you are to remain in this grown-up life. There is, of course, a catalogue of Implausible Yet Effective Excuses to Avoid Going to a Meeting, which you should carry around with you at all times, particularly to prepare yourself for those unscheduled meetings that managers like to spring on employees to make sure they're still alive.

Oh God, you know what? I'm actually having a vagina transplant at two thirty and I mustn't be exposed to large table clusters for 24 hours beforehand.

Oh, the joys

Becky says things about ...

... the dentist

The Tooth Attacker. The Oral Bandit, the Ivory Pirate. Whether you like it or not, Readerbuddy, life dictates that a) you have to go to the dentist; and b) there is no place for your dignity.

The trip gets off to an unhopeful start, as one look at the dentist's chair tells you that getting into it will not be calamity-free. The chair is reclined awkwardly like a lilo on a choppy sea, flanked by arms clutching a fearsome surfeit of lethal instruments, protruding wires, and highly expensive, breakable equipment. The only method of sitting down is to perform a bizarre and ungainly backward shuffle, involving your bottom pointing obnoxiously at the dentist's face, followed by a little jump, and an impact of your posterior with the chair that sounds like a hippo fainting.

As if this weren't traumatic enough, you've then got to open your mouth. Wider than the anatomical limitations of your jaw will allow – but you've still got to do it.

Once admitted access to your face, the dentist becomes your Oral Overlord. He has the power to peer into your mouth, think to himself 'Hmm... I'd much prefer upper 13 to be filled with lovely porcelain' or 'That faintly discoloured second molar would look far better round my neck,' and make tyrannical decisions about the future of your mouth. Guess what you can do about this.

Bugger all.

For who are you to question the dentist? Who are you to disagree when a trained professional advises that if you do not allow him to force a metal rod so far up your gum that it pokes out your eyeball, your teeth will rot, crumble, or explode (very unlucky), and leave you with crippling pain and unsightly swelling for life? Unless you have the knowledge to match theirs – and, as the well-known saying goes, 'No one has the dental knowledge to match that of a dentist apart from another dentist' – you really are in no position to quibble.

So once this Facial Fascist has decided which particular horrendous procedure he wishes to carry out on you, there begins a depressingly degrading process.

Your mouth will be numbed so that your lips feel like whale blubber. Pneumatic drills will be forced into your face – the sound of a steel tip cracking your precious pearly whites will haunt you for days – and a wordless assistant will suck up your uncontrollably gushing saliva with a small vacuum cleaner. And that is perhaps the worst thing of all: the silent judgement of the dental assistant.

Halfway through the ordeal you may be ordered to rinse. There is a slow, agonising, saliva-filled journey as the chair is made upright, and you swirl an unidentified neon liquid round your deadened mouth, dribbling 90% of it down your chin like a toothless old drunk, and what you hope will be a clean-cut spit into the basin turns into a half-retch, half-fling of stringy, phlegmy liquid that dangles from your lips like the miserable futility of your blackened soul.

And when you've been speared, stabbed, suctioned and dentally abused to within an inch of your sorry life, you must go through the dribbling rinsing process again – and then comes the hilarious punchline in this protracted and hellish sick joke.

That'll be £1,468,799,013 please.

Becky says things about ...
...the embarrassment of daily life

Sadly, my peach, life comes laden with shame. Observe:

You are in your local high street. Someone waves at you. You don't know them, but you wave back: after all, it is polite to return a cheery salutation. You then realise that they are waving at the person behind you. Embarrassment ensues. You take the only conceivable escape route, which is to immediately pretend you are receiving an important phone call, put your silent phone to your ear, and talk into it. There is no one on the other end of the phone, Readerpoo. No one. Just your own crippling indignity.

If there is anyone there, can you please send a herd of buffalo to stampede over me?

We all know that pretending to be on the phone solves a multitude of evils:

1) Someone is boring you to death. You need an ingenious escape. You reach for your bag or pocket. You say 'I'm *so* sorry, I just have to get this'. You walk away and have a conversation into a plasticy silence for three minutes, hoping that, by the time you return, the boring person will have forgotten what they were saying and talk about something more interesting.

2) You see someone you just *know* is either going to demand that money you've owed them for ten years, or will ask you *again* to go out with their perspiring brother. The phone comes out, the head goes down, and you embark on an intense conversation with *no one*. You may as well have some fun with this tactic to make sure it is ultra-intense and completely uninterruptable.

However, these sudden important phone calls are fraught with danger. Your phone **will** ring as you have it desperately pressed to your ear whilst absorbed in fervid conversation. Why is your phone ringing while you are having a conversation into it? Is there something terribly wrong with your device? Or is it because you're actually talking to an imaginary person in order to avoid having to talk to a real person? Yes. Yes it is. You socially awkward buffoon.

And what about the other embarrassments that plague our days? Have you run for a bus, missed the bus by a millisecond, and turned your desperate sprint for transport into a casual afternoon jog? Darling, of course you have. And what about that little accidental trip up a kerb? Turned that into a playful jog as well, didn't you? Thought you'd style it out and run a few steps like you were suddenly filled with the joys of life and had to expend some energy?

Every single day can be hampered by menace. You are crossing the road. The car at the crossing toots at you. You cannot ignore that toot. It is the toot that says 'The person who is driving this car recognises you as a chum and would like to greet you by utilising their automobile's mode of acknowledgement; furthermore, they demand a response'.

You give the car windscreen a cursory glance. Your worst fears are thus confirmed: **all you can see in the windscreen is a reflection of the sky.**

You have two choices:

1) Ignore the toot and walk on. When you are later faced with a pal who says 'Hey, I tooted at you earlier and you completely ignored me,' you say 'Oh, did I? Gosh, I'm dreadfully sorry, I must have been in a world of my own'. Crisis averted. You are an evil genius.

2) You throw caution to the wind and peer at the windscreen, squinting like there's no tomorrow, knowing full well that the person in the car is thinking 'Christ, she looks like a ruddy idiot squinting like that – she's known me 20 years, can't she see me? Why is she making that stupid face? Bloody hell,

she looks like an absolute dick, I wish I'd never tooted in the first place. Maybe I should just run her over and make this whole situation less awful for both of us. I could say I had a sneezing fit and accidentally slammed my foot on the accelerator. Oh, this is horrible.'

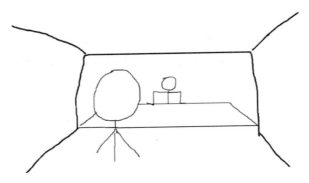

It is an appalling situation. The only method of escape is to simply run away, then deny you were ever on the scene. They can never prove it was you.

I've been trapped under my fridge all day and only escaped four minutes ago, so it definitely wasn't me.

It was definitely you. I know that, because I have eyes.

And bodies, buddy. *Bodies*. The very structures that comprise our existence are mortifying.

You nip to the toilet at work. You smile at Sandra from HR plucking her chin hairs in the mirror. You enter a cubicle. You sit down. A fart like a foghorn bellows forth into the aural receptors of everyone within a 60-foot radius, not least Sandra from HR whose hairy chin suddenly doesn't seem quite so embarrassing. You can do nothing but curl up into a toilety ball.

Gracious, is there a ship approaching?

The violent sneeze that releases a small but audible *vvvp* from your lower regions; the unexpected belch that erupts in the middle of a supermarket aisle and offends a nearby pensioner; the unannounced throat gurgle that growls like an angry tortoise in an otherwise silent office. Your body is your enemy. It is a foul, shameless noise machine with the sole intention of causing you social angst.

Dearest, these are the moments that make us the people we are. Let us laugh at ourselves and the social gaffes that bedevil our existence. And if you find yourself faced with a moment of particularly acute mortification from which you believe you cannot recover...

...that's just life, baby.

Becky says things about ...
... the madness of technology

What's that you say, my splendid associate? My mobile telephone can tell when I'm looking at it? How can an inanimate object tell when I'm looking at it? That's absurd! I've only just got used to the fact that some telephonic devices can *use a fingerprint to unlock them*. Readerboo, everyone knows that fingerprints can only be used to unlock things in spacey-future films, like *Men in Black* and *Star Trek*. In spacey-future films, fingerprints can unlock things like sliding doors that go *phhht* in neon corridors populated with immaculately made-up women with severe haircuts carrying clipboards and talking about xeno hackers infiltrating their nuclear centrifuges.

The thermonuclear propulsion system has failed – quick, your fingerprint is the only one that'll unlock this door.

I don't have a fingerprint – I'm a stick.

Technology is *mental*. Do you ever get pangs of nostalgia over a time when the most exciting thing in the world was getting your holiday photos developed *in a shop*? Or your dad letting you use the one computer in the house to play Chip's Challenge for half an hour before bedtime? Or spending hours trawling through the superb selection of screensavers on Windows '95 and realising you can make your computer screen turn into A LOT OF FLYING WINDOWS???

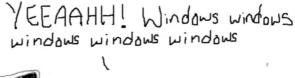

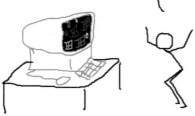

Everything now is so *slick,* so *easy.* What about the excitement of not knowing whether the printer would *actually print* your homework?

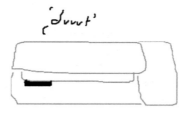

EXTREMELY LONG PERIOD OF SILENCE

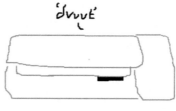

50

YET ANOTHER LENGTHY AMOUNT OF NOTHING

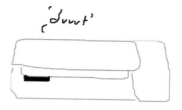

MORE SILENCE THAN YOU CAN EVER IMAGINE, UNTIL...

Or what about having to *work stuff out for ourselves*? Where is the fun in this:

Person 1: Have you ever wondered what the moon is made of? I mean, imagine if it were made of yoghurt, or ink, or tiny space-fairy wings woven together with the delicate webbing of interstellar spiders? Imagine if we discovered that everything we thought we knew about the moon was wrong, and it is actually made of *diamond*, and eventually some shrewd astronauts will chop up the moon and distribute bits of diamond to everyone on earth and we'll all be rich?

Person 2: Hang on, let me Google it... It's made of a solid iron-rich inner core and a fluid outer core primarily made of liquid iron.

Oh. We'll just forget that nice little imaginative speculation and sit in an all-knowing silence, shall we?

And the thrill of the household scramble to record TV programmes! The stern circles in the *Radio Times*, the obnoxious post-its on every surface yelling RECORD *PRIME SUSPECT*. The frantic last-minute dash fiddling with the ridiculously complex controls on the video player to ensure we had set the timings *to the millisecond,* and the tenterhooked anticipation of *whether it had actually worked.* A successful recording meant domestic harmony and televisual glee; a failed recording meant slammed doors, burned TV schedules, and histrionics over the sheer *crapness* of crude technology and everything it stood for.

But what do we do now? We wave the remote in the general direction of a peculiar and vaguely ominous box under our TV, and we can record *anything*. We can record *whole series*. No more fiddling, no more uncomfortable crouching in front of a video player and jabbing fingers at it in the hope that something will happen – we can walk outside our house, point the remote at a passing elderly lady, press one button, and *it will still work*.

And technology is only going to get more mental. Touchscreen mirrors, anyone? Yes, it's a thing. Forget being yelled at for getting your sticky fingers all over the bathroom mirror: technology has reversed the order of the Universe by *encouraging* us to swipe, prod and smear our grubby hands all over it. Your bathroom mirror doesn't need to be merely a useful surface in which to study that pesky spot or attack your eyebrows – it can show you the *news* or the *actual weather forecast*. You can answer emails, do online shopping, and check your bank statements, all whilst *brushing your teeth*. How much of an absolutely marvellous start to the day could that be?

Becky says things about ...
... school vs life

Ah, school days. The happiest days of your life. Over a decade of incessant learning. You'd like to think that those thousands of hours of lessons and homework actually come in useful in grown-up life, wouldn't you, my educated Readerpots? Well, let's see how useful they've been to my adult life so far.

Geography

Right, Geography, if you'd actually shown me a map of the world even *once,* it may have prevented my long-standing and deeply misguided belief that the Falklands were part of the Channel Islands.

I can, however, point to a picture of a river and correctly identify its source, tributary, confluence and mouth. I'm still waiting for the day when this skill may come in useful, but I'm sure it won't be long.

Maths

You are stuck in an Arctic ravine. It is 50 feet deep, you have been there for three days, you have severe frostbite and hypothermia, and you are close to death. You could really do with some help.

Then someone appears at the top of the ravine. At last! Aid has come! You get up on your crusty, frostbitten feet, ready to catch the rope, or abseiling equipment, or First Aid Box, or whatever incredibly useful item they are about to drop down to you.

They toss something into the ravine, you hold out your hands, and catch...

...a spoon.

The spoon is Maths. It has not been helpful.

Drama

It's true, Drama, I am confident in social situations, I have a great appreciation of the theatre, and you allowed me to stretch my playwriting legs on occasion, for which I am very grateful – but you know that time you made me lie on the floor with two of my classmates and pretend to be a pond? Bizarrely, I've not yet encountered a situation in which I can either re-enact this experience to my benefit, or draw from its important lessons learnt. Moreover, it has instilled in me a profound loathing of physical theatre and a wholly unreasonable disdain for the patrons thereof. So thank you, Drama, for making me so bitter at such a young age.

You absolute bunch of dicks.

German

You taught me to say 'My hamster has died' in your language. I waited for years to use this phrase, and when poor little Cliff eventually kicked the bucket, I was perhaps irrationally delighted.

Yeeahh mein Hamster ist gestorben!!

Information Technology

Sadly, with the breakneck and irreversible advance of technology, everything I learnt on an Acorn computer back in 1994 is now thoroughly defunct, and has left me with nothing but a peculiar nostalgia for floppy disks.

Physical Education

You taught me that if I move my limbs in a slightly faster manner than normal, it allows me to move quickly away from something. I believe this is what your textbooks call 'running'. This proved unfathomably useful that time I bumped into my old P.E. teacher.

English

Well, I conceive it to be of manifest unambiguity that my acquisition of a superlative proficiency in the English language has been capaciously utilised and resulted in an unsurpassed mastery of prose and semantic artistry notwithstanding heretofore thereafter circumambulate discombobulation antidisestablishmentarianism thesaurus.com.

Science

You have failed me in every conceivable way. The only word I can remember from Biology is 'photosynthesis' – just the word, mind, not the meaning of the ruddy thing; I can't wire a plug, I'm frightened by the phrase 'electromagnetic spectrum', and when my sister and I had a drunken New Year's Eve debate over which Science was responsible for the fizz in champagne, we settled on Chemistry, purely due to the presence of bubbles, and everyone knows that Chemistry involves many bubbles.

Art

I think my immense artistic skills speak for themselves.

From this extensive exploration, I have deduced two things:

1) I owe my parents an apology and a considerable amount of money; and

2) Life appears to be entirely manageable if you know how to say 'My hamster has died' in another language and have a steady hand with a mouse in Microsoft Paint.

Becky says things about ...
... getting old

If you look in most dictionaries, dearest beloved, you shall see that the definition of 'annoying' is thus:

> annoying
>
> *adj*
>
> someone younger than you complaining that they are getting old

At the time of writing this, I am 29 years old. I will be 30 very soon. Whatever your opinion of this fact – and yes, presents are definitely welcome, that's extremely kind of you – 30 years old feels older than a bug that got trampled by a diplodocus, spent 150 million years buried under layers of sedimentary rock, was discovered as a fossil in 1932, then spent a tiring 70 years being transported overseas to sit in a dusty glass case and be gawped at by tourists taking incessant photographs.

I'm too old for this shit.

Being nearly 30 brings with it a plethora of factors that result in us nearly-30-year-olds feeling ANCIENT. These factors are, in no particular order:

a) Telling someone how old you are and receiving the following response, accompanied by a playful shoulder nudge:

There is only one suitable reaction to this comment.

b) The undeniable presence of wrinkles. Not just those threadlike sweeps of character under our eyes, or the cute flicks of smile lines at the corners of our mouths, but deep, cavernous gorges. Frown-lines like daggers that scream 'I HAVE BEEN WORRYING ABOUT TURNING 30 FOR 30 YEARS'. That *terrible* moment we walk past a shop window, glance at our reflection, and see that dark trench of AGE furrowing from the inner corner of our eye and into our cheek like an unstoppable reminder of our impending and terrible demise.

c) The realisation that 30 years is a long time for our bones to be holding our body together, and, as a consequence, they don't work quite so well.

d) Being asked 'What did you do yesterday?' and, after a lengthy silence, during which we plough more depth into those frown-lines, replying 'I have no memory of yesterday.'

e) Where once we could spend happy hours perusing photos of our Facebook chums unconscious in club toilets or cartwheeling naked in the mud at Glastonbury, we are now faced with a daily barrage of baby photos, engagement announcements, wedding albums, blurred black and white photographs that make us think 'Why would someone post a picture of the inside of a plughole?' and then realise it is a foetus and that, at the age of nearly 30, it is perfectly acceptable, nay, *expected*, to own a foetus.

f) Never, ever, *ever* being asked for ID when buying alcohol. And, on the rare, wonderful occasion we *are* asked for ID, it is quickly followed by 'Actually, don't worry about it.' Why? Because they have spied our wrinkles, smelt the Deep Heat on our lower backs, and told our four children to get their hands out of the confectionary.

g) Congratulating yourself and your fellow ageing chums on arranging a night out at an *actual club* where you can *dance* and get *stupidly drunk on cheerfully-coloured shots with an unnecessary alcohol content*, and then sheepishly calling each other on the day of the event and making excuses like 'I've had *such* a knackering week at work,' or 'I just don't have the money at the moment, the new washing machine has wiped me out,' or 'London is such a *long way* and it's so *busy* and the club will be *so loud* and we won't be able to *talk*,' and you all end up going to the local pub for a nice comfortable chat and a sit down.

Chess, anyone?

h) Sitting in said pub and observing the antics of a group of people in their early 20s whom you cannot help but label in your aged mind as *youths*, and becoming irritated by their noise levels, their irresponsible drinking (*three* shots of Sambuca *each*? Who *needs* that?), their loud declarations of sexual and alcoholic conquests, and their carefree, worry-free, and wrinkle-free faces, which inspires a death rattle of bitterness from your table of over-the-hill curmudgeons.

Enjoy it while it lasts, losers.

And, at the age of nearly 30, we are faced with a most startling piece of wisdom:

NO ONE KNOWS ANYTHING.

We have spent our whole lives looking up to grown-ups and thinking how *wise* and how *all-knowing* they are, and we've been keenly awaiting the day when the grown-up switch flicks on, and we'll suddenly understand mortgages, or what a dividend is, or how to program a boiler or do a cryptic crossword, and become a proper, qualified ADULT. But, our 30 years of experience in the ridiculous world of humans have finally taught us that 99.99% of grown-ups are simply fumbling their way through life, trying to make enormous decisions, behave responsibly and look like they know what they're doing – when in fact they still stub their toes on bedposts, fall over whilst putting on their underwear, get nervous talking to their boss, and struggle with supermarket trolleys.

I don't understand why it won't just move in a straight line.

So, there really is only one thing for us nearly-30-year-olds to do: just carry on.

Learn how to cover up our wrinkles, accept that we can no longer sit cross-legged for an extended period of time, keep making mistakes, ignore the Facebook foetuses, persevere with the cryptic crosswords, and make sure we are never too far away from a nice cup of tea and a custard cream.

Girls and boys

Becky says things about ...
... what happens inside a lady's brain whilst shopping

CALAMITY. I have *nothing* to wear. My clothes are an insult to me, and to humanity. I'm going shopping. I'm going to buy a whole new wardrobe that'll totally revamp my image and make me look sophisticated and Hepburny and elegant, and everyone will go 'Oh gosh, Becky, you look so glamorous yet serene, let me contact *Vogue* immediately.' And I don't care about the money. I'll put it all on my credit card and cry about it later.

Onward!

Heavens to Betsy, shopping centres are busy. Where do these people come from? No matter, I can handle it. These suffocating crowds are no match for my determination to transform myself into a fashion icon.

Okay, first shop.

That top's nice... No it isn't.

That top's nice... No it isn't.

That top's nice... No it isn't.

That top's nice... No it isn't.

That top actually *is* nice! Glory be! I'll try it on. But I can't go to the fitting room with just one item; that's like only eating one crisp. That dress is nice. Not what I'd normally go for, but hell, isn't that the point? I'm reinventing myself! I'm Madonna! I shall treat clothing with whimsy and caprice. Dress, top, and let's go for that smart cotton jacket. Hang on, what's this? A random patch of leather on the back? What is this madness? It's fine, stay calm. It's edgy. Just like me. I am dancing on the razor-thin cusp of the avant-garde; I can handle a haphazard and wholly inappropriate leather patch. Maybe I'll add leather to all my clothes. An enigmatic trademark that says 'Am I kinky or do I just enjoy equestrian sports?'

God, this queue for the fitting room is unspeakable. Patience, sweet one; fashion takes time. Yes, three items please, you brooding, hostile Keeper of the Fitting Room. Don't worry about smiling, I wouldn't smile if I had to spend my days untangling women's pathetic attempts to put bras back on hangers the way they found them.

It's so hot in here I think I might die.

That looks awful.

That looks awful.

That looks awful.

Right, thank you, Keeper of the Fitting Room, and yes, all three items are now inside out, and that's a small lesson about the unfairness of life.

I shall not be disheartened.

Maybe I aimed too high. Let's try another shop. This one looks hip and trendy, let's try here.

Oh, these clothes look rather funky, I'll certainly be upping the funkometer here... hang on, these clothes are almost *too* funky... oh dear *God* I've wandered into a haven for funky teeny boppers! Oh, great shoulder pads from hell, everyone is 14 years old! I have to get out of here – but I can't simply turn round and walk out because it'll look like I've just realised I'm way too old for this place, which is of course exactly what I've just done, and people will either assume I'm a tragic late-20-something who is desperately trying to cling on to her youth, or I've come in to buy something for my teenage daughter, but I'm clearly still fairly young myself, which would mean I had my daughter *very* young and therefore was a teenage slutbag, and PRETEND PHONECALL, yes let's delve into my bag for my completely silent phone, and let's look peeved as though I've been interrupted from some excellent shopping, implement an irritable 180 degree turn, and let's get the ruddy buckets out of here and go and find something more age appropriate.

This shop is much better. Full of grown-up women who have hit puberty and pay car insurance.

Oh, that dress is *perfect*.

What the...? I don't understand. There are straps and holes and bits everywhere. How does it work? I'd have to be shaped like a coffee table to get into that. Who designs these things? Is this some kind of sick joke? And what are these insane psychedelic patterns on everything? And leggings! Leggings everywhere! Oh yes, I'll definitely look brilliant in a pair of incredibly skinny leggings splattered with asymmetrical patterns. Oh no wait. I won't look brilliant at all. Because I have a BOTTOM. I'd look like a juggernaut in a tarpaulin.

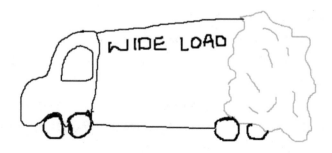

This is intolerable.

Last shop, and it's either success or death.

Now that *is* a nice top: sleek, sophisticated, a lovely shade of sapphire... oh, you like it as well do you, incredibly elderly lady? Yes, it's nice isn't it? The colour will complement your blue rinse beautifully. That's right, toddle off to the fitting room with the top with which I was going to adorn my not-yet-30-year-old torso.

I have the taste of a 90 year-old. Thought that was funny, did you, adolescents sniggering by the much younger clothing? You won't laugh forever.

Support pants are never far away, you smug little shits.

This has been a fucking disaster.

I shall spend the rest of my life a tragic fashion catastrophe, and I shall forever wear that black top that I bought in 2007 and which has holes under both arms, but if I don't lift my arms to catch any passing balls or to show an expression of joy, I'll get away with it.

I still really want to spend some money. Anything. I just want to be involved in a monetary transaction. I could buy a shower curtain. I need a shower curtain. If I can't make myself look pretty, at least I can make my bathroom look pretty. Maybe I'll make an edgy dress out of my old shower curtain. Maybe I'll just go home and cry into a tin of tuna.

Becky says things about ...
... men and menstruation

COME BACK, BOYS!

As well as being a writer, Reader, I am also a lady. I've been a lady for a while (nearly 30 years – did I mention that?), and this experience has led me to consider an important social phenomenon: the curious relationship between men and the monthlies. Allow me to elaborate.

Whilst at work one day I was quietly groaning at my desk, due to the fact that (WARNING TO MALE READERS: IMMINENT MENSTRUAL DESCRIPTION) my pelvis and abdomen felt like they were being stapled to a piece of rusty metal and ground with the heel of an industrial boot. My male colleague asked me what was wrong. Too weak to come up with a man-friendly reason for my whimpering, I muttered 'Time of the month'.

'Oh bloody hell oh God oh blimey oh Christ,' he gabbled, turned a shade of red deeper than the blobs of womb lining oozing into my knickers at that very moment, and supersonically changed the subject to a work-related topic; but, really, he may as well have done this:

Such was the severity of his revulsion at this natural process; a process which, I am led to believe by the experts, is fairly common, endured at some point by 50% of the world's population, including *all* the women that are of sentimental value to my male colleague, and literally *every single woman* to ever pass within a 4,000 mile radius of him. It could be said that he is positively *besieged* by menstruation. In fact, if it weren't for the miracle of clothing, he could, at any point, be surrounded by this:

Despite the prevalence of menstruation in society, my colleague's reaction is not uncommon amongst menfolk, and is one of, I believe, four types of male reactions to this foul female habit.

The first reaction is that detailed above: those dudes who consider a menstruating woman to be a dirty, contaminated she-beast, plagued by a contagious disease that can infect the men if they stand too close.

These men will recoil in horror at the mention of a mere womb twitch. They cannot hide their disgust. Their wives, girlfriends, mothers, sisters and daughters all become members of a malevolent sorority that gets together every full moon and relishes in its nefarious power to endlessly bleed. These men know that we women take up this revolting habit on a monthly basis, but they can't fathom why we don't just *stop it*. To combat this evil mystery, they take solace in their own razor-sharp wit by saying **hilarious** things like 'Never trust something that bleeds for a week and doesn't die.'

On a scale of 1 to 10, the potential for this joke to backfire on them if they make it in the presence of a menstruating woman is approximately 2,503.

(NB to the ladies: never trust something that is stupid enough to make a joke about not trusting something that bleeds for a week and doesn't die within earshot of a woman who has been bleeding for a week and hasn't died.)

The second male reaction to menstruation is mortification. These gentlemen would rather walk around in a t-shirt that says 'I CAN'T ACHIEVE AN ERECTION' than be anywhere near a period conversation. Even words associated with periods are too much for them to handle.

Tampon.

OhmyGodohmyGod
ohmyGodohmyGod
ohmyGodohmyGod
ohmyGodohmyGod
ohmyGodohmyGod
OhmyGodohmyGod

Their main problem with this horrific and intrinsically female process is that it involves two concepts coming together in a marriage they can neither accept nor bring themselves to contemplate: vaginas (which they like), and blood (which they don't). The very notion of it will send them trembling into a corner until they can think about something else.

Vaginas and blood
Vaginas and blood
Vaginas and blood
Vaginas and blood
Vaginas and blood
BEER.
Ah, that's better.

The third reaction is to simply pretend that periods don't exist. An innocent 'It's that time of the month' comment to one of these men results in 'We don't need to talk about that,' and a seamless continuation of the previous conversation. It doesn't matter how obviously they are faced with the truth: these men will deny the very existence of menstruation.

Petrol's gone up again.

The fourth reaction is a fairly rare one: those men who are *actually okay with the whole thing*. These heroes put the men in menstruation. A woman is always delighted to find one. Believe it or not, fellers, it's actually a very attractive quality. I'm not saying it's a total deal-breaker, but it helps.

He did say he wears a coat made from his mother's leg hair, but he's okay with periods so he can't be all that bad.

These chaps are so laid back that when we girls moan about our wombs feeling as though they are about to slip through our vaginas like a rotting jellyfish, they say, without batting an eyelid, 'Oh dear, that sounds painful. Do you want a paracetamol?' These champions should be applauded.

Of course, the intricacies of menstruation aren't necessarily something that dudes *need* to know about, and when we're crying at dog food adverts and complaining that our colons are throbbing, we must forgive them for being a trifle perturbed. But some men take a 'need to know' attitude to extreme levels: I once had to correct a male chum who, it transpired, thought that tampons came in different sizes in order to cater for different-sized vaginas. I gently pointed out that, were this the case, it would be rather difficult to market the 'Super Plus' range.

Oh boys, I can hear you shouting 'Stop having a go at us! Why do you women insist on *talking* about it???'

Put it like this: imagine that every month your testicles shed their skin, and turn into two seeping, excruciating, bleeding sacks of doom. It is traumatic. You want to get the trauma off your chest; you want to talk to someone who *understands*. So you talk to Steve, or Frank, or Barry, whose testicles do exactly the same every month.

We women share this common ground, but with our wombs, not our testicles. We like to check that our friends suffer the same level of agony. And yes, we have zero qualms about going into detail, because when you've woken up in this state –

– you have literally no shame left.

Becky says things about ...
... being a rubbish woman

Dear Womankind

You're welcome. I gave you the fun body. You get the boobs, the glossy hair, the hips, the squidgy bum. I hope you enjoy it, because I really put a lot of effort into it.

All the best, Universe

Dear Universe

Thank you. You're right, this body *is* fun. I sometimes find myself squeezing my own bum, like a stress ball. It's comforting. But I fear I'm letting you down, Universe. I don't think I'm very good at my body. The complexities of being a woman are, frankly, ridiculous.

For example, you've given us all this hair. What are we supposed to do with it? Some women handle it beautifully: they have sleek business-like 'up-dos', fringes that sit happily at their allocated angle, whimsical corkscrew curls, all delicately constructed with pins and clips and grips that create fountains of coiffured abandon – whilst I sit under the humdrum melancholy of a frizzy ponytail.

Nobody knows the troubles I've seen.

I have *tried*, Universe. I have meticulously followed YouTube tutorials, I have bought contraptions and equipment more reminiscent of open heart surgery than casual grooming; I have come dangerously close to breaking my neck as I contort my body in front of the mirror to achieve what bottles and tubes promise will be *INSANE VOLUME* and *COMPLETELY MENTAL BOUNCE.*

I even bought thermo rollers. I was determined to acquire a tousled-dramatic-Emily-Brontë-mermaid look. I followed *all* the instructions. I practically *became* the instructions. After 20 minutes, I unravelled the rollers in quiet anticipation of the twirled glory to come, and achieved the following:

Gravity, you are a cruel mistress.

Before   After

What about *nails*, Universe? I don't understand how we're supposed to keep these nails looking presentable. I can't operate nail files, I can't afford constant manicures, and stick-on nails are surely for the under-18s or over-80s. I *yearn* to be able to drum my gleaming talons on a desktop, or drape my hand elegantly across my neck to show off my French tips. My nails look like a hobo's teeth. Ragged, torn, unkempt finger teeth. How will I ever find a husband with nails like that?

I give you this ring as
a OH GOD LOOK AT
         HER NAILS

And *facial contouring*? What are you trying to do to us?! Why did you give us faces that need to be contoured? Aren't they three-dimensional enough? How three-dimensional do you want them to be?

Looking good.   Thanks, you too.

Those chicks on YouTube casually slap orange bronzer all over their mugs, and before I can say 'Oh gosh, someone should tell her she's put on way too much and she looks like someone's tried to draw a map of the North Circular on her face,' they do something flicky and sweepy with an enormous brush, and they are transformed into an airbrushed delight! I am filled with confidence at how *easy* it is, and I attempt to do the same. Except it's not that easy, Universe. It's never that easy.

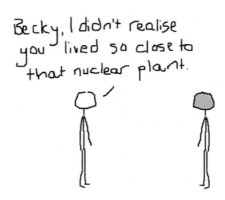

Becky, I didn't realise you lived so close to that nuclear plant.

Our delicate skins need moisture, Universe. I would *love* to be that girl who lovingly swathes her limbs with creamy goodness morning and night, and slips about the world an oiled nymph, un-plagued by the dreaded freckling of dry skin on tights, or the raw, chapped knuckles of a cruel winter. And I would love to remember to *exfoliate*. I want to buy a loofah and *use* it, instead of have it mock me from its untouched position in the bathroom cabinet, a devilish symbol of my *failure* to remove my billions of dead skin cells and reveal the nubile smoothness underneath. I want a life that is not tormented by that silently watching loofah.

And the *social expectations*, Universe. Women are supposed to be able to darn. I can't darn. I have never mended a piece of clothing in my life. I cannot thread a needle. I have tripped over a thousand hemlines, I have trailed them in the mud and hoisted them up round my knees, and I have never once thought 'Maybe I should learn to darn'. Why? Because I fear the delicate peril of a sharp needle would be rendered lethal under my ham-fisted oafishness.

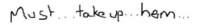

For you have created a monster, Universe. Were you expecting a graceful, swanlike creature, gliding through life like a dawn mist? Well, I'm sorry. I am the most inelegant, elephantine lummox to walk the earth. I cannot do anything daintily. I make more noise performing everyday tasks than a troupe of Morris-dancing rhinos. Cupboard doors bang. Tupperware clatters to the ground, bins tip over, windows break, mirrors shatter, roof slates explode, children cry. I get so caught up in the whirlwind of my hulking ineptitude, that it's almost a surprise to find myself in a wasteland of devastation caused by the fact that I am a hopelessly maladroit bint.

I have never cleaned my oven, flowers perish in my presence, I do not own an iron, I drink lager from the bottle instead of a ladylike G&T from a tumbler, I obsessively watch *Man VS Food* instead of *The Great British Bake-Off*, I forget my eyebrows exist, I sneeze like a warthog farting, I leave socks lying around, I don't know my bra size, I hate ponies and rabbits, and I have never mastered lip liner.

Universe, I am sorry. I'm trying, I promise to try to be more –

Oh.

Blimey.

Nobody's perfect

Becky says things about ...
... bad habits

Comrade, I have a confession.

When I was a child, I used to pick my nose and wipe the contents on furniture; namely, under the arms of the sofa, under tables, on the carpet.

If you haven't flung this book out of the window in disgust whilst muttering 'That Becky is a repugnant excuse for a human being, and I'm sorry I ever spent money buying her probably snot-encrusted tome', I am eternally grateful. I promise that this tome is not snot-encrusted, and I have not wiped nasal deposits on items of furniture for at least two decades.

For this was indeed a terrible habit; but, my cherub, the world is full of people doing terrible things, like not showering for three days, or urinating on toilet seats, or smothering a plate of grilled salmon and stir-fried pak choi with ketchup, or drinking seventeen cups of coffee a day.

I still have plenty of bad habits. I crack my joints: knuckles, neck, back, ankles, wrists, eyelashes, tongue, hair follicles, anything on my body that can bend. I take the booze train to Tipsy Town more than I should. I twiddle my hair incessantly, which isn't necessarily a bad habit, but its flirtatious connotations have the unfortunate consequence of making literally everyone think I want to have sex with them.

But I'd like to think that innocently twirling my silken fronds round my digits isn't as bad as, oh, I don't know, SPITTING.

When you are enjoying your lunchtime prawn sandwich on a park bench, is there a sight more repulsive than some evil individual hacking up a load of phlegm and projecting a great hunk of mucus onto the pavement by your left foot? No. There isn't.

Of course we all get the occasional displeasing backlog of saliva – particularly on a cold day or after a run – but most of us are content with *swallowing* it. Yes, I know it's disgusting. Sometimes it feels like an oyster, and yes, occasionally, you feel like you should have chewed it first, but nevertheless you should never, *ever* inflict your gunky mouthal build-up on another human being. I have committed this heinous spitting crime only twice in my life, both times after a run, and both times my spit ricocheted off the air and exploded back onto my chin. Serves. Me. Right.

Mother of God

In fact, releasing anything from your body into the public arena is a pretty foul habit. Everyone farts. There isn't a human being alive who hasn't released a small wind biscuit into the atmosphere whilst queuing at the bank. Everyone has performed the slight elevation of a bum cheek to let go the pressure of lower internal vapour. We've all freed a potent and audible gust whilst enjoying the sudden hilarity of a particularly amusing joke.

It wasn't that funny.

But is there any need for a trouser cough at dinner? Is there call to release fetid stenches into the convivial atmosphere of a pub? Will I ever recover from the day when I was ascending the platform steps of Wimbledon station behind a businessman and, just as I was at precisely face-to-bottom level, he farted in my face as I was yawning? If you've ever wondered what the inside of a colon tastes like – which, by the way, I have not – then I am sadly equipped to inform you.

Answer:

Like shit.

But a bottom bomb is a treat when faced with more calculated bad habits.

A scenario: you put the washing on. You get an unexpected phone call advising you that there is a rare natural light display in Inverness. You pack up your valuables and spend three days in Inverness observing nature's wonders. After three days you return, and remember your washing. You open the washing machine door. A stench like the bottom of a putrid pond billows forth. You have two options.

1) Wash the load again, tut over the extra 73 pence you have spent on water and electricity, but take comfort in the fact that you shall traverse the world a fragrant, heavenly human being.

2) You think 'Oh well', remove the mouldering laundry, let it dry, and traverse the world a rank, rotten specimen that will nasally offend everyone who comes within 400 feet of your rancid being.

There is no excuse for this, and yet the sheer amount of malodorous individuals encountered in day-to-day life is astonishing. An ill-timed deep breath in front of the tinned soup in Sainsbury's can make for an unpleasant experience if the person next to you is malodorous.

And, as if we needed help with bad habits, advancing technology provides us with a multitude of evil practices that we can utilise on a daily basis.

You do something productive, like writing nine words of a chapter for your soon-to-be-published blog book, and congratulate yourself by spending the next two hours on Facebook. You take yourself out for an evening stroll in the cool crepuscular air, and the entire walk is consumed with your nose glued to your phone and you walk into three trees and a badger. You settle down to watch that documentary on the revolution of steam that you were really looking forward to, and spend the programme answering emails on your iPad and not learning anything about the importance of steam to the modern world.

And whilst many humans can resist the urge to bite their fingernails so that they spurt blood into their chocolate digestives, or can fight the craving to consume that whole sharing bar of chocolate over three hours of reality television, it seems that *no one* can defy the incessant temptation of needlessly swiping at their phones instead of gazing out of a train window or enjoying a real live conversation. Commuters ogle their phones for entire journeys. *What are they doing?* you muse. *Are they playing some wonderfully compelling game or learning about modernist confessional poetry?* No. They are merely staring at their home screens, desperately trying to think of something to do on their phones to prevent them having to just *think* inside their own wretched heads.

I know, I'll change my volume setting from 'loud' to 'normal.'

Yes, we are a loathsome bunch. Filled with gruesome noises, smells, and dubious behaviours. Why can't we all just be pleasant, aromatic individuals who

Parp.

Sorry.

Becky says things about ...
... hangovers

What's that you say, blossom? You have no concept of hangovers, for you merely consume the purest of vegetable essence with maybe a drizzle of tree sap if you're feeling skittish? Nonsense. Don't tell fibs and stories, you deceitful souse.

Like life itself or the aftermath of a takeaway curry, hangovers can be unpredictable. They can be merely a mild irritation – no more bothersome than a slightly sunburnt elbow – or they can be a catastrophic event that forces you to reassess your very existence.

Okay, okay ... I wasn't put on this earth to drink ... From now on .... oh God ... from now on I'll just KNIT.

Sometimes the sheer meekness of a hangover can be a stupendous victory that makes you feel like a superhero with a liver of titanium (I believe they call that particular superhero 'Low-Density Corrosion-Resistant Major Organs Man'). These hangovers should be celebrated, Readerballs, for you are clearly bionic. Go forth and drink dangerously and to excess!

These hangovers sometimes wonderfully occur after those silly nights when you start on the beer, have a few cheeky wines, some bright spark suggests Jägerbombs, and before you know it you've got your face in a bucket of Tequila and someone is preparing a syringe with which they mean to inject absinthe into your larynx, and you wake up the next morning to nothing but a slight headache and an ambiguous stain on your lapel.

And when those nights of absinthe-injecting and Tequila-inserting do catch up with you, and you wake to cataclysmic devastation, a cat is on fire, barbarians have invaded and children have perished, you don't mind so much because you know you ruddy well *deserve* it.

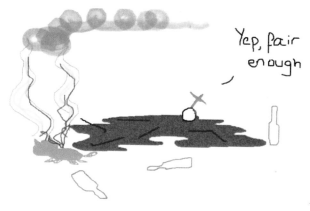

But sometimes your body doesn't want to play. Sometimes it says 'Hey, you. Person that I keep alive. You shall pay for this boorish over-indulgence, you hear me? I will end you.'

After a hard day at work you think to yourself 'I'm going to imbibe a couple of well-earned alcoholic beverages because I have been productive, efficient and generally smashing today, and what harm can a mere two glasses of wine do to my most excellent body?' You pop down the pub. You consume said two beverages. You go home and you go to bed. It is a perfectly pleasant evening.

And then you wake up and feel like this:

Your first emotion is an intense wish to die. Your second emotion is confusion. Why has this happened? Why do you hurt so? Who hates you? Surely you only had two drinks?! This crippling pain could surely only be the result of consuming thirty glasses of Rioja, mugging an old lady, stealing her pension and using it to buy Special Brew and White Lightning, consuming this in a bush, gate-crashing a student party and achieving a record for sucking the contents of a bottle of vodka up your bottom, flying to Dublin, draining a whole village of its Guinness, flying back, and getting hit by a transit bus carrying holidaymakers to their plane to Malaga.

These hangovers are unfair. They are perverse. The ratio of fun to pain is deeply unbalanced. A malicious force is wreaking havoc on your innocent body. These hangovers are not to be trusted. They make you doubt yourself. They make you think you are destined to a teetotal life of perpetual alcohol refusals.

Hangovers taunt your stomach. One minute you are gorging on fried pig and two loaves of bread, and the next you experience the Sudden And Categorical Certainty That You Will Vomit If You Move Your Body Even A Millimetre.

For the love of God, stick to the vegetable juice.

Becky says things about ...
... failed exercise attempts

EXERCISE.

Sorry, I didn't mean to startle you, petal. I shouldn't boom connotations of physical activity at you when all you're doing is sitting on your bottom reading a silly book.

I too like sitting on my bottom. Tremendously. I also quite like exercise. I get occasional waves of enthusiasm for it. Who doesn't enjoy the immense smugness of sweatily getting into a shower after a 30 minute run?

But for every 30 minute run, there is a Failed Exercise Attempt. You know what I'm talking about, my little static Readerpants. Those carefully planned workouts, that picture of the perfect body pinned to your wardrobe, the delicate fillet of lemon sole in your fridge, everything geared towards transforming you into the Most Awesome Example of Physical Flawlessness in the World Ever. All going up in smoke like a tea towel left on a burning hob.

Your hopes
and
dreams

Through my extensive experience of this subject, I have identified four types of Failed Exercise Attempts and, because I adore you, I shall detail them here so that you don't have to get up and experience them for yourself. You're welcome, honeybunch.

The Unexpected Failure

You spend all day looking forward to a Really Good Workout. You imagine your flushed cheeks, your ripped abs, your toned thighs, your peachy buttocks. You bound home with the confident stride of a winner. You observe Rule No. 1 of a successful after-work exercise session – DO NOT SIT DOWN EVEN FOR ONE MOMENT – you leap into your sports gear, which you lovingly laid out on your bed that morning, you crank up some banging tunes on your iPod, you hop into the evening light, you take those first sprightly steps in your new running shoes, ready to run for hours and miles and miles and hours ...

... and the truth smacks you round the love handles like a slimy trout.

You really cannot be arsed.

What the
fuck am
I doing.

You try everything: you tell yourself you are fat and disgusting, you grab fleshy handfuls of your inner thighs, you search frantically through your running playlist for a motivational tune... but it is all in vain. You just can't be ruddy bothered.

You lope home, turning the air blue with your curses, you rip off your sports gear, kick your new trainers at the wall, and you order a pizza and spend the evening watching atrocious television in a vile immovable torpor.

FAILURE

The Expected Failure

You just *know* it's going to end badly. You taunt yourself with jeers of 'Oh right, going to exercise, are we? Really? Yeah, good luck with that. We'll just see what happens. You are a laughing stock.'

You go through the whole sorry rigmarole of putting on your tracksuit, selecting your running playlist, chuckling sadistically to yourself; you stomp outside, you take an ironic little jogging step...

...and the whole thing unravels with a tiresome inevitability.

You spend three hours eating ice cream in front of YouTube, but you tell yourself that it's okay because you *expected* to fail, so you haven't actually failed at anything *per se* because you succeeded in meeting your expectation to fail, and you open the second tub of ice cream to celebrate your astute self-awareness.

The Gallant Attempt

Likely to occur in gyms, where the pressure is most acute.

You have a promising start. You get a bit moist on the bike. You go *really fast* on the cross-trainer for two minutes, which probably burned about

3,000 calories because you were going so *unbelievably fast.* You plod for a bit on the treadmill. You look at the chest press, and note the *intention to* use it. You know you're on a knife edge, and you can feel eyes on you. Cruel eyes. Judging eyes.

You pull yourself together, you stride across the gym, you grab the weighty-arm-strengthener-handle-pully thing, you give it an almighty tug with the strength of an ox in his prime...

...and it hurts slightly, the gym is just so *stuffy,* your shoes are rubbing, you're thinking about dinner, and life's too short.

You scuttle to the changing rooms, splash some water over your face to give the appearance of sweaty success, and you drive home in a car that is powered by your own self-loathing.

The Non-Attempt

You lie on your bedroom floor intending to do 100 sit-ups.

You do two.

You get up and go to find food.

My cherished, immobile little gum-drop, there really is only one solution to these abhorrent physical failures:

Have a sandwich.

Becky says things about ...

...rage

You have inhaled the foul gasses of wrath. You have plunged into the waters of ire. You have gorged from the table of umbrage. The stimulus of your gall may be something harrowing and profound, like a back-stabbing friend or an unfaithful lover; or, it could simply be one of life's Moments of Inexplicable and Disproportionate Rage at a Minor Incident. These are the inconsequential things that send a normally laid-back person into a torrent of spleen. Everyone is plagued by certain sparks that light the fuse of unjustifiable fury, and, if you will permit me, my treasure, I shall exhibit the most powerful of mine.

People Unnecessarily Reading Out Words

Individuals who feel the need to vocalise every single word they see around them make me unaccountably livid. This peculiar rage was cultivated by an elderly acquaintance who, on car journeys, would read out loud *every single road name and every single billboard and every single shop sign we passed.* What would you do in this situation, my love? Hmm?

Exactly. You would set fire to your own foot.

Imagine. An entire car journey filled with a relentless commentary of geographical wordage. It was as though she went into some form of signage trance, saying dreamily 'Gloucester Road... Herne Drive... Craven Street... Tesco's... Boots... Vision Express... Starbucks...'

And with every vocalisation, I would sit in the back seat wishing that this lovely, innocent woman would have a sudden heart attack.

People Who Dawdle At Ticket Barriers

We all know that terrifying moment of panic at approaching a station ticket barrier: *What if I don't find my ticket in time???* Normal people step to one side where our physical presence will not be an obstacle to others, and we rummage in our bags and pockets, cursing wildly under our breath, until we find our ticket and join the hordes of folk through the barriers. All is well. Except that not everyone is normal. There exist rancorous offspring of Beelzebub in this world who choose to search for their missing ticket *in the entrance to the ticket barrier.*

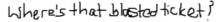

I tell you what, Satanic Toad searching for your ticket at the ticket barrier, why don't you just sit down and have a rest while you're there? Got a button that needs sewing on? No problem, I'll fetch you a travel-size darning kit and you can mend it right there. You brute.

Irrelevant Detail In Stories

Being told a story is a lovely thing. Whether it's humorous, sad, or sphincter-looseningly exciting, it should be a joy. However, so many verbal tales are ruined by narrative detours of such despicable irrelevancy that they make me want to run headfirst into brickwork.

Behold the following scene:

Brenda: Did I tell you about when I found a body in the airing cupboard?

Verity: No? Gosh that sounds exciting. Pray tell.

Brenda: One Wednesday I'd just got home from work – or had I been to yoga? It could've been ballet conditioning, actually... perhaps it was Thursday, in which case it would've been Pilates. Anyway, I got home and – no, it was definitely Tuesday because I had my swimming kit and my hair was wet – unless it had been raining – I know we'd had a lot of rain, because I remember saying to Gary how the marigolds would suffer...

Brenda: Anyway, I got in and made myself tuna pasta – or was it salmon? No, definitely tuna, because we hadn't had any salmon in the house for ages because Sainsbury's had been out of it for about two weeks – could've been a month, come to think of it, I know it was a good long while... So I ate my pasta, had a glass of water and an apple, maybe even a banana, although I don't tend to have bananas in the evening because they give me gas, and I took some washing out of the washing machine... or was it the tumble dryer? I think I put another load in, you know, jeans, shirts, socks...

Brenda: ...and I took some ironing upstairs – we'd just had Ian and Bev over to stay, so I'd had extra linen to iron, and the new steam iron had packed in and we'd had to go to B&Q to get a new one – ninety quid, can you believe it? Gary was furious. Yeah, so I'd gone upstairs with this pile of ironing, which had taken me all Saturday morning to do... or had I done it Sunday? It could've been Sunday because I think we'd gone to Gary's mother's and she'd made this awful marmalade tea loaf – or was it a lemon drizzle?

Reader Reader Bang Bang, I do not have it in me to endure such flagrant contempt for narrative pertinence.

And recounting those things has sent me into such a bluster that I shall be forced to smash myself in the face with the picture frame that I bought from Debenhams. Or was it John Lewis? Actually I'm pretty sure it was eBay...

Becky says things about ...
... Becky Says Things

My Reader. My friend.

We have reached the end of our journey together. We have delved into this ridiculous life with zest and panache; we have experienced the joy and trauma of our existence, and we have come out the other end. We are brave soldiers, you and I. Crusaders of life.

As I mentioned, a lot of the stuff in this book originated in my blog, beckysaysthings.com. I started this blog in March 2012. I deliberately chose a pleasingly vague title for the blog, because I wanted to do just that: say things. Free rein to chat about everything from hangovers to periods to how much I hate people who dawdle at ticket barriers? Yes please!

I started drawing pictures to add some flair to the things I said, and these silly little pictures soon evolved into –

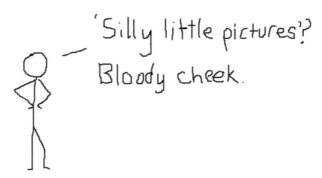

'Silly little pictures'? Bloody cheek.

Oh blimey, you've piped up. Okay, Stickman, you are more than a 'silly little picture'. You are an exquisite pictorial tool with which to illustrate the profundities of life. I suppose I should introduce you, as you've stuck your oar in – Reader, Stickman; Stickman, Reader. He helps me say things occasionally. You might have noticed him.

Au contraire, Sticky. I can categorically inform you that you would quite literally be nothing without me and my proficiency with a cordless mouse.

So after two and a half years of saying things on my blog, my lovely and loyal readers started telling me I should turn it into a book – and I thought, why the bobbins not? And, because HarperCollins was on holiday and Penguin was engaged, I decided to publish it myself.

I spent weeks in front of Microsoft Word, writing, re-writing, editing, re-editing, drawing, re-drawing, designing, formatting – and if you've ever tried to do anything in Microsoft Word that involves section breaks and page numbering, you will know that it **literally makes you want to kill yourself** – and here it is. The fruits of my labour. My magnum opus.

And by reading it, you have helped make my dream come true: I want to be a fully-fledged, proper writer, and a large part of achieving that is having readers. That's you. And I need your help.

I would not be writing this book, my blog, or indeed anything, without years of feedback and constructive criticism from people who have read my work.

So I want to hear from you.

Look at this lovely email address:

beckysaysthings@gmail.com

Use it to tell me anything. Tell me whether you thought the book was:

a) Absolutely pant-wettingly hysterical
b) A jolly good effort
c) Mildly amusing
d) Barely worth the use of your eyes
e) It is now being used to stop the washing machine from rubbing against the new paintwork in the utility room.

Anything. *Anything!* Tell me how I can improve. Tell me what I did wrong, what I did right. Tell me where you bought this book, or who gave it to you, and whether you're going to lend or recommend* it to someone else to spread the silly joy. Anything will help. I can't go anywhere without you.

And finally, thank you. Thank you for reading my first self-published book, and thank you for supporting the dream of a nearly-30-year-old who wants to make people chuckle.

---

* Please recommend it. I've got 200 copies of the bastard thing.

Thank you

Becky has wanted to be a writer forever. She studied English and Creative Writing at the University of East Anglia; then a few years later, after realising her various jobs as a barmaid, teaching assistant and office administrator weren't quite what she wanted to do, she did a Masters degree in Creative Writing and Publishing at Kingston University. She was lucky enough to get a book of short stories published with Treehouse Press in 2011 (you can buy *Lost Souls* on Amazon), and has been working on a novel for more years than she cares to reveal, but is determined to finish it in 2015. She currently works as a freelance project assistant to the NHS, and would very much like not to be doing that for the rest of her life. She is also a freelance copyeditor and humour writer. She is mildly obsessed with Marmite, enjoys a good sandwich conversation, and her dream is to spot someone reading her book on the London Underground.

I can't believe you're writing about yourself in the third person.

Shut up, Stickman.